Please Walk Beside Me

A GUIDE FOR CONFIRMATION SPONSORS

JOSEPH MOORE

Paulist Press
New York/Mahwah, N.J.

Library of Congress Cataloging-in-Publication Data

Moore, Joseph, 1944–
Please walk beside me: A guide for Confirmation Sponsors / Joseph Moore.
   p. cm.
Includes bibliographical references.
ISBN 0-8091-9580-1 (alk. paper)
   1. Confirmation—Catholic Church. 2. Sponsors—Handbooks, manuals,
etc. I. Title.
BX2210.M584 2004
264′.02082—dc22

           2003020978

Published by Paulist Press
997 Macarthur Boulevard
Mahwah, New Jersey 07430

www.paulistpress.com

Printed and bound in the
United States of America

Contents

Introduction

If you are to be a sponsor for a confirmation candidate, this booklet is for you. While it is primarily designed for sponsors of younger or older adolescents, there is much that will also apply to you as a sponsor for an adult, or even for a young child. You can read these pages privately in order to benefit your relationship with your confirmation candidate. You can also discuss what is written here with other sponsors by using the discussion questions at the end of each section. You are about to embark upon a spiritual journey with another Christian Catholic who has asked you to walk beside him or her. This does not mean you have to have all the answers about the Catholic faith. What it does mean is that someone is looking to you for support, spiritually and humanly. This is a time to grow in your own faith as you help another person to become fully initiated into the church. Begin your journey with a prayer:

> Spirit of God, enlighten me.
> Grace of God, move me.
> Heart of God, electrify me.
> Compassion of God, touch me.
> Hand of God, heal me.
> Passion of God, stir me.
> Mind of God, counsel me.[1]

1

So You Have Been Asked To Be a Sponsor?

So you have been asked a big question by a young person: "Will you walk beside me in my journey? Will you walk beside me in my journey of faith, in my journey of life, at least for now?" And what was your reaction to this request? Did you find it flattering, or scary, or challenging, or embarrassing? What emotion did this invoke in you? I know a young man, Peter, thirty years old, who was asked by one of his students to be a sponsor. Peter was hesitant because he did not go to Mass every Sunday. Peter thought he might be the wrong person to ask. I also know a woman who was moved to tears when her niece asked her to be a sponsor. People have all kinds of reactions. Once in a while it is better to say that you think it would be a mistake for you to be a sponsor, but ninety-nine percent of the time it is not. Even if you think you fall short of the norm of the ideal Catholic, it may be appropriate for you to take on this role. Being a sponsor can reawaken or refresh your own faith. So often I have seen a young adult who has left the church for a while return with heartfelt devotion when one of his or her children is baptized or receives first holy communion. So don't be too quick to eliminate yourself! Be gracious and respond affirmatively right away, or else ask the young person to give you a little time to think about it, or pray about it, or to discuss it with someone who can give you good advice.

What does it mean to be a sponsor anyway? We will examine that question from various angles in this booklet. The Latin root of the word *sponsor* means "to promise solemnly." At confirmation, what are we promising then? In a sense, we are promising to take on a responsibility. This responsibility has to do with someone else's life—not their *whole* life, but a part of it. A sponsor in a twelve-step recovery-from-alcohol problem is promising to try to help another person remain sober. With the sacrament of confirmation, a sponsor is promising to walk with another person in his or her faith journey. It is the same promise made at baptism by godparents. That is why we read in the *Catechism of the Catholic Church*: "Candidates for Confirmation, as for Baptism, fittingly seek the spiritual help of a sponsor. To emphasize the unity of the two sacraments, it is appropriate that this be one of the baptismal godparents" (1311). We will talk more about the relationship between these two sacraments, and we will also discuss who else may be a sponsor besides godparents.

This promise you are making by accepting the role of sponsor goes beyond promising to participate in a parish sacramental program. Although that is a part of it, it is a deeper, more encompassing promise. It is saying that at this particular point in the life of this young person, I will be there beside them to encourage and support them in their Catholic faith. It is saying that I will also accompany them in their struggle to find meaning in life and to find God. Being asked to be a sponsor is

truly a wonderful invitation, because in the effort to help someone else in their life of faith, your own faith will surely grow.

Another role for a sponsor, aside from promising this walk
of faith, is often that of mentor. This is usually because of the
age difference between the sponsor and the confirmation candidate. Mentoring is a lost art in society today. People are paid
to be mentors in some places! When I was a child I remember
taking a quarter that someone left on a table in the ice cream
parlor I used to go to with my friends. It was supposed to be a
tip, but the waiter had not seen it yet. His name was Mr.
Waters. He was not only the waiter but he was the counter person and the pharmacist all in one, in his dusty old drug store. I
remember high, high shelves with packages of ointments and
bandages and pills. Mr. Waters had to use a ladder to get at
much of the merchandise. That's where he was when I quickly
swept that twenty-five cents into my pocket. Well, I did not get
away with it. Mr. Waters did not see me, but Miss Madigan, a
bank teller in town, was seated at another table behind me and
my friends. "Joseph," she admonished, "put that quarter back
exactly where it was." This loud remark caught Mr. Waters'
attention. Everyone in the ice cream parlor looked at me. My
face turned red and soon I felt as though I was wearing a scar-
let letter. By the time I reached home, Mr. Waters had tele-
phoned my mother. I felt as if the whole town was looking at
me because I was a thief. And since that day when I was ten
years old, I have never stolen again.

They say it takes a village to raise a child. This is what we
today call "mentoring." It means helping someone to grow and

develop. It means taking responsibility for the moral welfare of both the community and the child. Sadly, today mentoring seems to have vanished from our land. I was standing beside our pastor after Sunday Mass recently when a woman came up to him complaining that another parent had asked her child to be quiet during Mass. "How dare someone else correct my child!" Do you understand what I am saying about today's culture? People are actually *afraid* to point out the misbehavior of anyone who is not their own flesh and blood. People are afraid to admonish teenagers—afraid that there will be retaliation, or that their own safety will be jeopardized. This is a sad state of affairs; however, it is our reality. We need people now to form intentional relationships with young people in order to be able to constructively criticize them. Being a sponsor will involve you in this forgotten art of mentoring.

There are very few good, moral role models for children and young people today. Celebrities are often wrapped up in a very materialistic lifestyle; politicians have been exposed in the media for corruption; athletes fight with each other on the field and some have been charged with the use of illicit drugs. It is hard to find a hero today. It seems to me as though public figures are not able to fill that void. More and more, I believe children are looking for heroes right within their own circle of relationships. More than ever young folks are looking for adults who are genuine, honest, generous, selfless, and brave. Don't be surprised if your confirmation candidate looks up to you in some way! If he or she did not, they would not have chosen you. Heroes today are, in a way, "nobodies" instead of celebrities—"nobodies" just as Jesus was.

In most dioceses across the United States, the rite of confirmation is celebrated during adolescence. However, the *Catechism of the Catholic Church* states that the sacrament may be received by children in danger of death, but that normally it should not be received until at least the "age of discretion" or reason (1307). We determine this age of reason to be about seven years old, and in some dioceses you may be asked to be sponsor for a child who is that young. That is because those dioceses are restoring the order of the reception of the sacraments of initiation as it was in early Christian times: baptism, confirmation, and Eucharist. Some dioceses celebrate confirmation at the end of the middle school years, and others during high school. Adults who never received confirmation when they were younger, or who are just becoming members of the church, may also ask you to be a sponsor. If the adult (called a *catechumen*) is participating in the Rite of Christian Initiation of Adults (R.C.I.A.), you would be asked to be a sponsor not only for confirmation, but for the entire process of Christian initiation. These individuals will culminate their entry into the church with the reception of all three sacraments of initiation during the Easter Vigil Mass. There is much in this booklet that can also apply to being the sponsor for an adult.

Confirmation is sometimes called the "sacrament of Christian maturity." This is especially significant for teenagers and young adults who are, in a sense, ratifying their own baptism. As outlined in the *Rite of Baptism for Children,* baptism is followed by a long period of faith formation. The purpose for this is so that the children can eventually "accept for themselves the faith into which they have been baptized" (*Rite of Baptism of Children*, no. 3). There is a debate among theologians about the proper age for confirmation. Some say it should follow baptism and others say it should be delayed until late adolescence. Our job is not to enter—let alone end—this debate. Our task is to live with the reality before us. Whatever age your candidate is, that is the age that God is calling you to be with.

If young people are being asked to confirm the baptism that was chosen for them as infants, they accomplish this in various ways. They can deepen their own relationship with God. They can enter more fully and more faithfully into the life of their parish community. They can make prayer and scripture and service more a part of their lives. They can come to understand Roman Catholicism in a more mature way. All of these are a part of the process of deeper initiation into Christ and his church. This is the process your confirmation candidate is asking you to share. It is a time in which both of you can learn more about your faith; both of you can become more active members of the parish community; both of you can grow in prayer and ministry to others.

The church requires that a sponsor or godparent shall "stand" for the person being confirmed. It is understandable that a baptismal godparent could fill this role when you view confirmation as the completion of baptism. However, with the separation of these two sacraments from infancy to childhood or adolescence, it may not be best to have a godparent as a sponsor. Why? Because godparents were chosen by parents and guardians and those particular individuals may not be attractive to a young person as a companion on his or her faith journey. Many times godparents are chosen to honor relatives of the infant, or they are friends of the parents, and this has little to do with nurturing faith.

A sponsor ought to be someone of faith who has already been confirmed. Let's look at that word *faith* for a moment. When we talk about the Catholic faith we often are referring to a body of beliefs, a set of dogmas that Catholic people accept as true. Faith can mean a belief that something exists. But more profoundly, faith is a way of living life and walking the journey we share because of trust in God. It is living life in such a way that even through all of life's difficulties, we know that nothing can separate us from God. It is not something that we acquire once and for all; rather, faith is something that we continue to grow in, all of our lives. When God told Abraham in the Bible to lead his people to a new land, Abraham had no map; he had no idea where he was going. But he listened to his heart and the movement of God's spirit within him. So his faith was not only that he believed in the existence of the one, true God, but that he was willing to trust his God as well. Faith cannot be passed on solely through CCD classes or religious education. Faith is not material that we have to learn and memorize. Faith is passed on by *people* who have faith, by a faith-filled community. The saying goes that faith is "caught, not taught."

Anyone can study about a religion and its beliefs, but that does not make that person a person of faith. Who, when you were young, was a person of faith for you? I remember an elderly, single woman in our parish named Alice. Every day at five o'clock in the afternoon she would drop into church to pray the Stations of the Cross. When I had my paper route we often crossed paths. One day I asked her why it was that she went to church to pray the Stations. With her blue eyes twinkling she looked down at me and said: "So that I can remember how Jesus suffered, when I have my own troubles, and to remind me that God never gives us more problems than we can bear." That simple answer, and the witness of this woman at church every single day, taught me more about faith than any book or class could have.

Even though church law allows a teenager to be a sponsor, it is probably not appropriate in most cases. If we have developed in our theological understanding of the role of the sponsor, we see the sponsor not only as a companion, but also as a mentor. We see the sponsor as someone who is a little further along the road of life and of faith than the confirmation candidate. One Catholic writer I know of could be talking about a confirmation sponsor when he discusses what it is to be a "minister" to someone else: "one who attempts to put one's own search for God, with all its moments of pain and joy, despair and hope, at the disposal of those who want to join this search but do not know how."[2]

Some people are not able to be sponsors because of certain obstacles that stand in the way. These include

- If a person is not a fully initiated member of the Catholic Church

10

- If the person is fully initiated into the church but has other issues (called "canonical impediments") such as being divorced and remarried outside the church.

For example, Jennifer wanted to ask her Aunt Cynthia to be her sponsor. Cynthia was baptized into the Catholic Church as an infant, and she received the sacraments when she was a child. However, as an adult, Cynthia never went to Mass except at Christmas, and to attend occasional funerals. She believed in the existence of God, but was not a member of a community of faith. Jennifer was very disappointed when the confirmation director in her parish advised her that her aunt would not be an appropriate sponsor. The director explained that it was not at all a judgment about her aunt. Maybe Cynthia was very close to God and lived a very good life. He acknowledged that Jennifer looked up to her aunt for the good qualities that stood out in her character. While Aunt Cynthia might be a good mentor for her niece in many ways, the role of sponsor should be asked of someone else. Cynthia would only be appropriate if she was herself in the process of a return to, and a deeper immersion into, her Catholic faith. If Cynthia's journey was taking a turn back into the church, then maybe it would coincide with Jennifer's journey. In that case, they could walk the road together. Otherwise, it would not be fitting. As the director pointed out, you would not ask a golfer to mentor you at tennis. Adolescents can benefit from more than one mentor. Another person as sponsor does not negate the role that Cynthia plays in Jennifer's life. But the mentor-sponsor is a person who is fully participating in the life of the church. It is someone who receives the sacraments regularly, and who tries to remain faithful to the beliefs and practices of the Catholic Church.

It is possible to look up to a spiritual person of another faith, or even to someone who has no religion to which they subscribe. Many human beings walk a holy path. However, the path of Jesus Christ, in the context of the Roman Catholic Church, is a journey with a faith-focus and a rich spiritual heritage. It is for this particular journey that a person needs a sponsor. Sponsors are not chosen to flatter or honor someone, nor are they chosen solely as a sign of respect and admiration. Sponsors at confirmation are chosen because they have something to say with their lives about how to be faithful to Jesus Christ and his church. Sponsors offer encouragement, support, and example in the journey of Christian faith.

(In case you are sharing a discussion with other confirmation sponsors in your parish, look for questions in this booklet enclosed in boxes. These will provide you with an opportunity to reflect together on the material you have just read.)

Who were your baptismal godparents? Are they still living? Do you have a relationship with either of them? What is that relationship like today?

CHAPTER TWO
About the Rite of Confirmation

In the Acts of the Apostles in the Bible, we read what happened after the Samaritan converts had been baptized by Phillip the deacon.

> Now when the apostles at Jerusalem heard that Samaria had accepted the word of God, they sent Peter and John to them. The two went down and prayed for them that they might receive the Holy Spirit (for as yet the Spirit had not come upon any of them; they had only been baptized in the name of the Lord Jesus). Then Peter and John laid their hands on them, and they received the Holy Spirit.
>
> Acts 8:14–17

From this and other passages in the New Testament, we learn that there was a rite in the earliest ages of the church, distinct from baptism, in which the Holy Spirit was conferred by the imposition of hands. We also notice that the idea of anointing with holy oil is commonly associated with the giving of the Holy Spirit. For example: "But it is God who establishes us with you in Christ and has anointed us, by putting his seal on us and giving us his Spirit in our hearts as a first installment" (2 Corinthians 1:21–22).

Recall the story of the apostles huddled in the upper room after Jesus was crucified. Forty days after Easter, on the feast of Pentecost, they were all filled with the Holy Spirit, and later left to go preach about God's great deeds (Acts 2:1–4). It is from these events as well that we recognize the coming of the fullness of the Holy Spirit as a special occasion.

The ceremonies for baptism and confirmation were influenced by Roman bathing practices. In second century Rome, a person's body would be rubbed with oil after their bath. In a similar manner, the bath of baptism is followed by the anointing with oil afterward. We have continued the use of oil or chrism at confirmation, as well as the laying on of hands. The confirmation candidate receives the mark or seal of the Holy Spirit. It is the completion of the sacraments of initiation and the strengthening of baptismal grace. For adolescents baptized as infants, confirmation is also a personal ratification of their earlier baptism. According to the *Catechism of the Catholic Church*, additional effects of confirmation are:

- it unites us more firmly to Christ
- it increases the gifts of the Holy Spirit in us
- it renders our bond with the Church more perfect
- it gives us a special strength of the Holy Spirit to spread and defend the faith by word and action as true witnesses of Christ. (1303)

Can you see now how baptism and confirmation are so closely connected? Baptism restores God's grace to us that was lost through the original sin of Adam and Eve. Confirmation seals us with the Holy Spirit, strengthening the grace of baptism. At one time we said in the church that confirmation made us "soldiers of Christ." Today we do not see military language as a way to talk about Jesus, who was a peacemaker. But the idea of being stronger in Christ remains true.

The way confirmation takes place is for the bishop or priest to extend his hands over the head of the candidate. Then he lays his hands on their head, anointing the forehead with oil. As he does this, he says: "Be sealed with the gift of the Holy Spirit." Oil is a sign of consecration, a sign that we are totally dedicated to Jesus Christ.

The *Catechism* mentioned that at confirmation we have the gifts of the Holy Spirit increased within us. The seven gifts of the Holy Spirit are: wisdom, understanding, counsel, fortitude, knowledge, piety, and fear of the Lord (it is not that we are "afraid" of God, but we have a respect for and stand in awe of God). The tradition of the Catholic Church also speaks of the "fruits," or results, of having God's Spirit within us.

> The fruits of the Spirit are perfections that the Holy Spirit forms in us as the first fruits of eternal glory. The tradition of the Church lists twelve of them: charity, joy, peace, patience, kindness, goodness, generosity, gentleness, faithfulness, modesty, self-control, chastity. (*Catechism of the Catholic Church,* 1832)

For discussion:

Did you notice any changes in yourself when you were confirmed?

Which fruit of the Holy Spirit would you like to see flourish more in your life?

CHAPTER THREE
What Qualifies You To Be a Sponsor?

If there are no obstacles to your being a sponsor, what qualifies you beyond being a fully initiated Roman Catholic? The first answer is that someone has asked you to be a sponsor! That young person obviously sees you as having something to offer, even if you cannot see it yourself. You need to trust that perception and accept the invitation graciously. It may well be the Holy Spirit speaking to you through this young person!

Jamie was in the eighth grade, and when time came for his confirmation preparation he did not know where to turn to find a sponsor. He lived with his mother who suggested he ask one of his uncles. But Jamie did not feel right about that. His uncle lived on the other side of the country and Jamie only saw him at family weddings and funerals. His mother's friend, Joanne, was someone who Jamie saw as being "cool." Joanne was in her late twenties and single, and she worked in town. Joanne was always the first to show up when Jamie's mother needed a babysitter, or help with anything for that matter. She was involved in the "Big Sister" Program in the community, and Joanne took her "little sister" out faithfully every weekend. Jamie also saw Joanne every Sunday at the ten o'clock Mass, where she played in the parish folk music group. Jamie knew there was something special about Joanne even though he could not tell you in words what it was. He felt a little funny about asking her to be his sponsor because it would add more duties to Joanne's already busy life. Eventually he got up the courage to ask her, and Joanne was overjoyed. She told Jamie that she felt very honored and Jamie knew he had made the right choice.

Even though you may in no way see any comparison between Joanne and yourself, recognize that the young person who asked you probably does. In some way, perhaps unknown to you, you are seen as somebody special. So enjoy that honor! However, there is something quite different about being asked to be a sponsor and being asked to attend a football banquet in a parent's place. Being a sponsor does involve guiding someone else who is growing in his or her faith. This can be quite scary. We may say to ourselves: "Why me? What do I have to offer? I'm no saint! What right do I have to tell someone else how they should live?" Even parents, whose duty it is to guide their children, feel very inadequate at times.

These feelings of incompetence are not to be feared; they are signs of humility that is based in truth. Most of us are not exceptionally holy or spiritual people. We live ordinary lives, with ordinary struggles and ordinary accomplishments. We are not theologians or priests or members of religious congregations. That's okay! A theologian is not what this young person needs right now. He or she needs a Christian adult who may only be a step or two farther along the road of life—a Christian adult who has the generosity to give of his or her time and gifts, whatever those may be, to help this young person walk the journey of faith. Think for a moment about the people who have helped you, both in the past and in the present. Have you chosen them for their academic degrees in psychology, sociology, or theology? Or have you chosen them because they make you feel affirmed, accepted, and listened to? I'd wager it is the latter.

Young people today respond to adults who are authentic, who are "real." They also respond to adults who help them feel good about themselves by their warmth, their acceptance, their love. If your confirmation candidate is a teenager, take that into account and remember from your own life experience that adolescence was a time when we were figuring out who we were—and forming our identity as a unique person. Of course we all do this our entire lives, and right now you are trying to figure out what it means to be a sponsor. Identity is achieved through self-acceptance, by knowing it is okay to be ourselves. We need to know that we are lovable in order to feel God's love. Obviously, your candidate must already feel accepted by you. This faith journey together will provide the opportunity for the young person to share with you at a deeper level who he or she is. By so doing, the youth's own identity will become more solidified. You will be able to reinforce what is good and to challenge what needs reform or development. Think of Jesus who accepted everyone in such a beautiful manner, especially those who were the most outcast in Jewish society: the lepers, the prostitutes, the tax collectors. This is the fundamental way in which people learned about God's love.

19

You are not alone in this quest to help young people feel loved and understood. Parents and guardians are certainly involved in this process as are teachers, coaches, and counselors. The parish too needs to play its part. Young Catholics need to feel a sense of belonging at church, a sense of being "at home." "Interviews with young people who have 'left the Church' often reveal that many don't feel they have left, but that they never belonged."[3] Youth ministry is the task of the entire community and you are one special individual in that community. We are engaged in the art, the gift, of affirming each other, challenging each other, boosting self-esteem and the feeling of being loved.

For discussion:

When you were a young person (or younger than you are now), what adult did you look up to, and why?

CHAPTER FOUR

What About Christian Service?

Jesus calls us into discipleship; he asks us to follow him. We follow Jesus as journeyers, as pilgrims in search of life's purpose. We receive our identities as Christians at baptism. "Baptism is birth into the new life in Christ" (*Catechism of the Catholic Church,* 1277). We are "reborn" in a spiritual sense, or "born again," as some would say. Dietrich Bonhoeffer was a theologian in Nazi Germany who was imprisoned and martyred. He wrote several books, the most powerful of which may be *The Cost of Discipleship.*[4] In it, he calls people back to the radical faith of early Christian times. Bonhoeffer believed that when Jesus calls us to discipleship, he gives us an identity, *his* identity. The unique characteristics of this identity are found in Jesus' Sermon on the Mount in the New Testament.

"Blessed are the poor in spirit, for theirs is the kingdom of heaven.

"Blessed are those who mourn, for they will be comforted.

"Blessed are the meek, for they will inherit the earth.

"Blessed are those who hunger and thirst for righteousness, for they will be filled.

"Blessed are the merciful, for they will receive mercy.

"Blessed are the pure in heart, for they will see God.

"Blessed are the peacemakers, for they will be called children of God.

"Blessed are those who are persecuted for right-eousness' sake, for theirs is the kingdom of heaven.

"Blessed are you when people revile you and perse-cute you and utter all kinds of evil against you falsely on my account. Rejoice and be glad, for your reward is great in heaven, for in the same way they persecuted the prophets who were before you." (Matthew 5:3–12)

These sayings of Jesus form the heart of the Christian life. The more we become the kind of person the Beatitudes speak about, the more we become like Jesus. One of the ways that many confirmation programs help candidates to identify more with Christ is through service or ministry. Christian service shifts our focus to what is important in life by dismissing power, fame, and riches. It is not all about us: it is all about others. When a young person is fully initiated into the Catholic community, they are say-ing, at some level, that they want to follow the radical path of Jesus' selfless service to others. Self-absorption is characteristic of our younger years (e.g., agonizing over that facial blemish that no one notices but us!). But service and ministry programs can begin to nudge the young Catholic into an awareness of the world and all its needs. By visiting an elderly housebound person, a hospital, a nursing home, a homeless shelter, a soup kitchen, a poor section of our own community—all of these contacts and experiences bring us into contact with the face of Jesus Christ. As a side bene-fit, they also propel us beyond our own selfishness. Sometimes the service is about charity or direct help to the needy, and sometimes it is about advocacy to change the root causes of injustice and poverty. Both are important. Jesus laid down his life for others, and in ministering to others, we too are laying down our own lives so that they may live more fully.

As a sponsor, you may be invited to participate in the service dimension of the confirmation program. It is a beauti-ful way to bond with your candidate. Seize the opportunity to do so, if it is there! If sponsors are not involved in the service component of your parish program, then your own lifestyle can serve as a model for your young person. Our actions will speak louder than our words. If we ourselves act like disciples of Jesus Christ, then we will be providing a powerful example. Another benefit of service programs that you can certainly reinforce is that they tend to break down barriers and preju-dices that we may harbor toward each other. By immersing yourself in a segment of society with which you do not usually come in contact, you can become a more open person. Divisions based on class, race, status, age, nationality, sexual orientation, and so on—all these can be overcome through simple human contact. As St. Paul preached:

As many of you as were baptized into Christ have clothed yourselves with Christ. There is no longer

23

Jew nor Greek, there is no longer slave or free, there
is no longer male and female; for all of you are one
in Christ Jesus. (Galatians 3:27–28)

Matthew volunteered to visit a seventy-year-old man who
was confined to his house in a wheelchair. His name was Bill,
and he had become an invalid twenty-five years ago after a seri-
ous accident. Matt went every Thursday around five o'clock
when he got out of basketball practice. He would give Bill's care-
taker an hour off, and then feed Bill the supper she had prepared
for him. Matthew did this for an entire school year, and he only
missed once when he had the flu. When he was confirmed in
May of that year, his service program was completed. But Matt
could not abandon his friend Bill. He continued to visit every
Thursday throughout his high school years. Today, when Matt
comes home from college, the first person he goes to see is Bill.
Bill has become, for him, the face of Jesus Christ.

When Mother Teresa was asked how we should help the
poor and suffering in the world, her answer was always the
same—to begin with one person. As the poet, Gerard Manley
Hopkins, put it: "Christ plays in ten-thousand places, Lovely in
limbs and lovely in eyes not his. To the Father through the fea-
tures of men's faces."[5]

For discussion:

What experience or which relationship in your life awakened your realization of the vast array of the needs of God's people? Have you had someone in your own life that was, for you, like Bill?

CHAPTER FIVE
About Prayer

Many of us in the Roman Catholic Church feel a little awkward about praying out loud or praying with another person. Outside of Mass, we have a long tradition of prayer as a private matter between ourselves and God. Some people—men especially, because our culture implies it is not masculine to share feelings—find it particularly difficult to pray with others. Prayer is deeply personal because it is the communication of our heart's deepest longings. Prayer is a two-way street: we raise our hearts and minds to God to ask him for all that we need, and then listen for God to speak to us.

> The Holy Spirit who teaches the Church and recalls to her all that Jesus said also instructs us in her life of prayer, inspiring new expressions of the same basic forms of prayer: blessing, petition, intercession, thanksgiving and praise. (*Catechism of the Catholic Church*, 2644)

Prayer of *petition* is when we ask God for something for ourselves: our need for forgiveness, or any other needs we may have. Prayer of *intercession* is when we ask God's help for the needs of others. Many of us spend our entire prayer lives in petition and intercession. It is important that we remember to *praise* and *thank* God as well. It is also important that we see prayer as a conversation with God. To do this, at times we need to listen as well as to speak.

How can we hear God speak to us? The Spirit of God speaks to us deep within our hearts. If we are attentive, we will feel the movement of the Spirit within us and will get more clarity on the direction we should go in life. We can hear God's voice in the voice of a friend who comforts us, in the voice of a hero who challenges us, in the voice of someone who loves us and affirms us. We can hear God speak in the awesomeness of nature: the mountains, the ocean, the peaceful meadows. But hearing God "speak" to us requires sensitivity, openness, and a discipline to still ourselves once in a while in order to *hear* God speak. Contemplation is a higher form of prayer where we make ourselves still in order to absorb God's love. There is a story about the Curé d'Ars, Saint John Vianney, an ordinary parish priest: One day he saw an old man seated in the back of his church. After a couple of hours, the Curé asked him if he was waiting to go to confession. "No," the old man replied, pointing to the crucifix above the altar, "I just look at him and he looks at me." This simple villager from nineteenth-century France summed up the essence of contemplative prayer in his brief reply!

You might begin a discussion of prayer with your confirmation candidate by sharing how and when you pray. You could talk about the difficulties you have in praying, as well as the benefits you discover there. If you are comfortable praying aloud spontaneously with your candidate, then by all means do so. But if you find yourself extremely uneasy about doing that, there are certainly other ways to pray together. You can hold hands and pray in silence; you can recite the Lord's Prayer aloud together. You can attend Mass or a prayer service together. You can promise to pray for each other during the coming week. It is really not important what *mode* of prayer you choose. What *is* important is to establish a spiritual friendship with your candidate by being, in some way, united in prayer. Perhaps the confirmation program in which you are involved will provide you with this opportunity. Following are ten tips on prayer—ten basic helpful hints about turning to the Lord:

1. Bring to Jesus your deepest needs and those of others. Save selfish or materialistic concerns for your own energy.

2. Accompany prayer with courageous human effort. As the old saying goes, "God helps those who help themselves."

3. Do not be superstitious when you pray. The prophet Elijah looked for God in the wind and fury of nature, but found him in a gentle breeze. The miraculous movements of God are interior and, most often, in the ordinary events of life.

4. Be persistent in prayer. Recall the gospel story of the man who got up from bed and answered the door in the middle of the night, not because he wanted to, but because the neighbor who kept on knocking was so persistent (Luke 11: 5–8).

5. Remember that sometimes prayer changes us instead of changing the situation about which we are praying. We

may *think* we know what is best for us, but God is the one who really knows what is best.

6. Prayer is a relationship that is built on trust. Even when you cannot feel God's presence, or it seems as though God is not listening, *trust* that he is there for you.

7. Read the Bible sometimes when you pray. Meditate on gospel stories and teachings by reading slowly, then close your eyes and think about what you have read, applying it to your own life. This type of prayer is called *Lectio Divina*.

8. Use self-discipline by setting aside three minutes of silence a day, at about the same time each day, when you still your wandering thoughts and focus in on God.

9. Pray in the manner that you find most helpful. You can pray in your bedroom, in church, outside—anywhere. If music helps to lead you into prayer, then use music. You can sit or stand or kneel, or use whatever posture helps you to pray best. God does not so much care *how* we pray, God just cares that we take the time to develop a close relationship with him.

10. Pray with others, especially at the Eucharist on Sundays. We need the spiritual nourishment the sacrament provides, as well as the support of a praying community. Pray the rosary. It is fine to pray alone most of the time, but we also need a community of faith.

For discussion:

What is your favorite way to pray? Where and when do you practice it? Do you believe that God answers all your prayers?

CHAPTER SIX

Some Problem Areas

As a sponsor, you may encounter some difficulties in walking this faith journey with your candidate. Older adolescents may be entering a stage which John Westerhoff calls "searching faith."[6] At this stage, there is an exploration of our earlier understanding of the faith of our childhood. This intellectual struggle for growth may be accompanied by difficult moments. What once made sense may not make sense now. One example would be that certain parts of scripture (for example, the story of Adam and Eve and creation) are now viewed as "untrue." The Bible cannot always be taken literally, that is word for word. This intellectual realization may shatter childhood notions and seemingly destroy faith. But faith is not destroyed by a more mature understanding of scripture. This confusion is only temporary. These are also years when adults, like parents and teachers, who once were seen as infallible (without flaws), are no longer seen as such. As we grow, we begin to realize that the people we admire have shortcomings. Hypocrisy is keenly observed by teenagers. A person who attends Sunday Mass and then acts in an uncharitable way during the week can be viewed as a hypocrite. This is because the young person has not yet learned to accept that we are all weak human beings; most important, he or she has not been able to accept the inconsistencies and failings in their own life. Your life journey might intersect with a young person's journey that is at this critical stage. Your confirmation candidate may even be rebellious toward reception of the sacrament. And this is okay too. Many times a caring adult who will listen to all of the growing pains of the adolescent is the key to growth. Do not be overly alarmed if this young person objects to being confirmed and says that it is being forced on him by his parents, or that he is only going through the motions. Be patient, and ask him to be patient also. Encourage him to simply be open as the two of you walk this journey at this point in his life. If after some period of time during the preparation for the sacrament there is no change (or further disillusionment), then perhaps the two of you will need to approach the pastor, or confirmation program director, about the possibility of postponing confirmation. My hunch is, however, if you can weather this storm along with your candidate, a more mature faith will eventually emerge. At the very least, do not be surprised or alarmed if you discover that, after consenting to be a sponsor, your young person is in a crisis of faith. It is an opportunity for you also to reexamine your own personal faith and for the two of you to grow together towards God.

You may also find yourself to be a sounding board for the confusion of adolescence, as well as for the very real concerns he or she may have about becoming more committed to the church. As we said, young people are discovering that adults are frail human beings who cannot always be held to the high standards that teenagers set for them. They may project this struggle onto the church, criticizing it for its failings or the failures of some priests or the hierarchy. You do not need to defend what ought *not* to be defended. Your task is to help this young person realize that we are a church of human beings and that God chooses the weak in this world to confound the strong. Sin has existed in the church down through the ages, but so also has the wisdom of the church been passed down. At any point in history—like the excesses of the Crusades or the abuse of selling indulgences in the time of Martin Luther—there have been problems in the church. But the glorious reality is that despite its weaknesses, the Holy Spirit is always with the church, protecting it from straying off in a direction other than that which God intended. "The Church in this world is the sacrament of salvation, the sign and the instrument of the communion between God and men" (*Catechism of the Catholic Church*, 780).

A young person may not always appreciate the collective wisdom of the church. The immediacy of our culture, where technology brings instant results, makes this appreciation all the more difficult. Again, you may become the dartboard for an adolescent's darts of confusion, impatience, desire for immediate gratification, and intolerance. You may also find yourself attempting to uphold a Christian principle, feeling very much under attack. If so, do not take the experience too personally. We get angry with, and lash out against, those people in our lives with whom we feel most secure. We have the assurance that these individuals will never reject us no matter what we do or say. It is indeed an art to be accepting and non-judgmental, while at the same time being consistent in our cherished beliefs and challenging to a teenager's limited perspective.

David, who was a senior in high school, told me that this was the best year of his life. He would graduate, he would be confirmed, and he would consummate a sexual relationship with a young woman for the first time. Lesson one: Do not betray your shock. I did my best to take his remark in stride. Lumping together confirmation and sex before marriage amazed me—but I was dealing with someone at a certain level of moral development. He was not at the same stage I am in terms of my thinking, my life experience, and my values. So I needed to accept him where he was in life and not to make him feel judged and/or rejected. At the same time, I needed to challenge him.

I said, "David, you are being confirmed into the Catholic Church. Do you know how the church views sex outside of marriage?" "I know," he replied, "but the church is from the Dark Ages on that. This is the twenty-first century and a lot has changed." So I affirmed the last part of his statement: "You are absolutely right, David, this is not the world that I, or your parents, grew up in—many things *have* changed." I went on to explain how a sexually charged media and culture presented an enormous challenge to Catholic values. It is difficult for young people not to think that everyone is engaging in sexual intercourse. I asked him if he saw any value in abstinence, and if he wanted this young woman, whom he thought he might marry, to be a virgin. We talked about the real meaning of intimacy being psychological, being exposed to someone who loves you for who you really are; and I pointed out that putting sexual intimacy before that level of trust and commitment was wrong. Of course, David maintained that the two of them had dated for three years and had achieved this emotional intimacy. I posed this question to him: "Why are you two planning to attend college in different parts of the country if your commitment is so profound?" I realized that David had an extremely unrealistic view of relationships. When he had a retort for every argument I posed, I had to rely on the wisdom of the ages. I told him that the church had good reasons for its position on sexual relations outside of marriage. I told him that even if we do not yet fully grasp the reason for things, sometimes we just have to *trust* in the collective wisdom of others. I tried to expose the traces of hypocrisy I saw in his commitment to the church through confirmation, while clinging to his own viewpoint in opposition to the church. Basically, I attempted to expand David's thinking about sexual morality. I talked calmly and did not yell or force my viewpoint on him. At the same time, I continued to echo what I thought and what the church's thinking was about the behavior he was planning. I was true to myself, the church, and to my mentoring relationship with him. I needed also to recognize that David might choose to ignore what I had said and continue to act in the way that he felt was okay. He may have to learn through mistakes. I am always comforted by the definition of *sin* we find by examining the Greek roots of that word. To sin meant to miss the mark, not to hit the bull's-eye, to fall short of the ideal. Sometimes we all fall short of our Christian ideals, but we pick ourselves up and try again to follow Jesus' way. To summarize, if you are confronted by moral challenges of either a personal (like sex) or social nature (like the morality of capital punishment), my suggestions are:

1. Try to remain calm.

2. Let the young person know that you have heard what he or she has said.

3. Do not be accusatory or judgmental in tone of voice.

4. Help the person to be realistic in the challenges you present.

5. Uphold your own values without hesitation, as well as the teachings of the church (no matter how old fashioned you may be accused of being).

For discussion:

Have you been in a discussion recently about a controversial topic? How do you behave when others disagree with you? Do you feel the need to win? Do you find yourself watering down your own convictions so they will be accepted by others? Is there a matter of Catholic moral teaching about which you are confused?

CHAPTER SEVEN

A Crash Course on Communication

I just spoke about David and his moral problem. I am wondering why he provided me with his information. He trusted me, I suppose, and wanted to see what my reaction would be to his statement. Being careful not to reject him or display horror at his remark, I began to use skills I had learned long ago. I began to use them without even realizing it; after a while they become second nature. I want to discuss those skills of being a good listener in this journey of faith, and although I will be referring to teenagers, the same skills apply for any age group (except very small children).

Let's start by addressing the "rescue fantasy." This means that when we readily identify with the pain of another, we take it upon ourselves to make them "all better." We have the temporary illusion that we can actually *solve* another person's problem *for* them! Let's use a little self-examination.

- Think of a problem you recently spoke about to another person (choose a real-life problem packed with emotion and confusion).
- What happened to you as you spoke about it? After you spoke about it?

- Who solved the problem, or at least reduced its stressful grip on you?

In ninety-nine percent of the cases, you will have answered something that went like this: "It made me feel better to talk about it, but I really had to solve it on my own." If this is the case with you, remember that this is so with those who approach you with *their* burdens. The Latin root of the word *compassion* is helpful here. It comes from *com patior*, meaning "to suffer with." Notice, it does not mean "I take away your pain, your doubt, your confusion." But in suffering with another in their difficulty, I do three things:

- I let them know they are not alone at this time.
- I, just by *listening* and *caring*, build up their coping skills.
- I become a sounding board, a backdrop against which they can talk freely, know that they are being heard, and have an opportunity to gain greater insight into a solution.

I do all this by just being a good listener! What I am doing is providing empathy and understanding by "walking a mile in another person's moccasins," as the old Native American saying goes. No one has to have all the answers. Sometimes I need to be listened to, and sometimes it is someone else's turn. It is a relief not to think we must have all of the experience, wisdom, and solutions to help out a friend or confidante. We simply need to be there.

Here are ten "commandments" for active listening that you can practice in speaking with your young friend:

1. Make eye contact with the person. If they are very shy and cannot look at you, be sure you focus your gaze on them (without "staring them down"). This gives them strength to speak. Try not to be distracted by what is around you.

2. Nod your head once in a while as they talk with you, or say things such as "I see" or "I understand" to show that you are following the conversation. Or you might ask them to clarify something they have said to you.

3. Keep the speaker on track. Don't interrupt by talking about your own problems.

4. Listen for deeper feelings behind the words or "between the lines." Trust your instincts about how the person is truly feeling, even if they make denials. Hunches are often accurate. State back to them the feeling you observe (e.g., "You seem pretty hurt by what she said"). In this way you can be like a mirror, helping them to see themselves more clearly.

5. Instead of asking questions which can be answered with a yes or no, use invitational-type questions to draw the speaker out (e.g., "Can you tell me how that made you feel?").

6. Do not act horrified or judgmental when given personal information. This is a tricky proposition, as we have dis-

cussed earlier. You are accepting the sinner but not the sin. You are being trusted with this information, so instead of lecturing them, try to draw them out to discover what they really feel about what has just been said. You are helping them to discover the truth that is inside them.

7. Don't use clichés for problems, such as "There are more fish in the sea," or "Tomorrow is another day." By using these, you are shutting down communication. You are saying something that everyone says, and this is not helpful. If you don't know what to say, then admit it. Remember, you do not have to have all the answers.

8. Do not provide advice unless it is really appropriate. You may relate to a young person's difficulties with parents, and you may wish to share what worked with you when you were their age. Or you may want to make a suggestion about how to handle negative peer influences. But never for a moment think that it is your job to solve their problems. In fact, if people don't find their own solutions, they will never really "own" them. If they follow your advice and it backfires, then it is your fault, not theirs (not in reality, of course, but in their way of thinking). A good way to frame advice is to begin with statements such as "What if you...?" or "Have you ever tried...?" And last, just like yourself when *you* have a problem, they are not so much interested in someone else's advice as they are in having you hear them out. This is what provides you with the vision to see more clearly what it is you need to do.

9. If you are having a conversation with them about something you have strong feelings about (e.g., capital punishment, abortion, or even whether or not a family should eat together every evening), acknowledge that, at least to yourself. If it is not an issue of morality but simply of preference or opinion, you need to be ready to suspend your own point of view. If you cannot, then be honest enough to say that you are not the best person to discuss this particular issue with.

10. Keep a person's confidence, because obviously you are being trusted. The only time you should break that confidence is if the young person has told you something that puts them at risk to themselves in some way, or puts others at risk (for example, if they are telling you they are going to try the drug Ecstasy, or that they intend to run away from home). The person you usually need to tell is a parent. Of course, you should tell the young person *before* you do that, because you need to break the confidentiality. But don't feel bad about it. You must recognize that the fact you were given this information in the first place is in itself a cry for help.

Please remember not to "play psychologist" here. Recall that psychotherapy did not exist before 1900. What did ages and ages of people do before that? My guess is that they went to trusted family members and friends to talk out their problems. Which ones did they choose? The same ones you choose; the ones who listen well.

For discussion:

Think about a time when you opened up about a personal problem to someone, only to discover that they did not seem to care or want to listen. What was your reaction? Who is the best listener you know?

CHAPTER EIGHT

The Rite of Confirmation

The rite of confirmation usually occurs within the Mass.

Presentation of the Candidates

After the readings, the bishop, the priest, and the deacons who will be ministers of the sacrament with him take their seats. The pastor or another priest, deacon, or catechist presents the candidates for confirmation, according to the custom of the region. If possible, each candidate is called by name and comes individually to the sanctuary. If the candidates are children, they are accompanied by one of their sponsors or parents and stand before the celebrant. If there are very many candidates, they are not called by name, but simply take a suitable place before the bishop.

Homily or Instruction

The bishop then gives a brief homily. He should explain the readings and so lead the candidates, their sponsors, and parents, and the whole assembly to a deeper understanding of the mystery of confirmation.

Renewal of Baptismal Promises

After the homily, the candidates stand and the bishop questions them: "Do you reject Satan and all his works and all his empty promises?"

The candidates respond together: "I do."

Bishop: "Do you believe in God the Father almighty, creator of heaven and earth?"

Candidates: "I do."

Bishop: "Do you believe in Jesus Christ, his only son, our Lord, who was born of the Virgin Mary, was crucified, died and was buried, rose from the dead, and is now seated at the right hand of the Father?"

Candidates: "I do."

Bishop: "Do you believe in the Holy Spirit, the Lord, the giver of life, who came upon the apostles at Pentecost and today is given to you sacramentally in confirmation?"

Candidates: "I do."

Bishop: "Do you believe in the holy catholic Church, the communion of saints, the forgiveness of sins, the resurrection of the body, and life everlasting?"

Candidates: "I do."

The bishop confirms their profession of faith by proclaiming the faith of the Church:

"This is our faith. This is the faith of the Church. We are proud to profess it in Christ Jesus our Lord."

The whole congregation responds: "Amen."

The Laying On of Hands

The concelebrating priests stand near the bishop. He faces the people and with hands joined, sings or says:

My dear friends:

In baptism God our Father gave the new birth of eternal life to his chosen sons and daughters. Let us pray to our Father that he will pour out the Holy Spirit to strengthen his sons and daughters with his gifts and anoint them to be more like Christ the Son of God.

All pray in silence for a short time.

The bishop and priests who will minister the sacrament with him lay hands upon the candidates (by extending their hands over them). The bishop alone sings or says:

All powerful God, Father of Our Lord Jesus Christ,
by water and the Holy Spirit
you freed your sons and daughters from sin
and gave them new life.
Send your Holy Spirit upon them
to be their helper and guide.
Give them the spirit of wisdom and understanding,
the spirit of right judgment and courage,
the spirit of knowledge and reverence.
Fill them with the spirit of wonder and awe in your presence.
We ask this through Christ our Lord.

Candidates: Amen.

45

The Anointing with Chrism

The deacon brings the chrism to the bishop. Each candidate goes to the bishop, or the bishop may go to the individual candidates. The one who presented the candidate places his right hand on the latter's shoulder and gives the candidate's name to the bishop; or the candidate may give his own name. The bishop dips his right thumb in the chrism and makes the sign of the cross on the forehead of the one to be confirmed, as he says:

"N., be sealed with the Gift of the Holy Spirit."

The newly confirmed responds: "Amen."

The bishop says: "Peace be with you."

The newly confirmed responds: "And also with you." [7]

(If confirmation is within the Mass, liturgy continues with the General Intercessions, Liturgy of the Eucharist, and the Final Blessing.)

Conclusion

Your young friend has now been initiated into the fullness of life in Christ and his church. He or she has received the Holy Spirit who comforts us and makes us holy. The Spirit also challenges us to spread the good news about Jesus Christ. As St. Paul wrote:

> For this reason I remind you to rekindle the gift of God that is within you through the laying on of my hands; for God did not give us a spirit of cowardice, but rather a spirit of power and of love and of self-discipline. (2 Timothy 1:6–7)

Confirmation is *not* a graduation or termination of a CCD Program. It does not have to mean that the spiritual friendship you have enjoyed with your candidate needs to end. As we have said, confirmation is the beginning of full membership in the church and of being empowered by Jesus Christ. Youthfulness is no excuse for failing to witness to God. Let us conclude with God's words to Jeremiah, a teenager, whom God called to be a prophet and speak out to the people of his day. Jeremiah complained that he was too young to speak out.

> But the LORD said to me,
> "Do not say, 'I am only a boy'; for you shall go to all

to whom I send you, and you shall speak whatever I command you. Do not be afraid of them, for I am with you to deliver you, says the LORD." (Jeremiah 1:7–8)

Confirmation Keepsake

Candidate's Name _____

Candidate's Confirmation Name _____

Date of Confirmation _____

Church _____ Place _____

Bishop or Priest _____

Notes

1. Moore, Joseph, *Prayers for a New Generation,* New York, Paulist Press, 1991, p. 6.
2. Nouwen, Henri, *Creative Ministry,* New York: Doubleday, 1971, p. 116.
3. Groome, Thomas, "Parish as Catechist," *Church,* Fall 1990, Vol. 6, No. 3, p. 25.
4. Bonhoeffer, Dietrich, *The Cost of Discipleship,* trans. R. H. Fuller, New York: Macmillan, 1957, pp. 89–98.
5. Hopkins, Gerard Manley, *Poems,* London: Humphey Milford, 1918, No. 34, "As kingfishers catch fire, dragonflies draw flames."
6. Westerhoff, John, *Will Our Children Have Faith?* New York: Seabury Press, 1976, pp. 94–96.
7. *The Rites of the Catholic Church,* New York: Pueblo Publishing Co., 1983, Chapter I, 38–44.